INTERROGATIONS

ALFRED ALLEN

Interrogations

SELECTED
POEMS

INTRODUCTION BY

Seán Lucy

TOWER BOOKS CORK

Published by Tower Books
86 South Main St., Cork

Printed in the Republic of Ireland
by Miros Press Ltd., 39 Lavitt's Quay, Cork

ACKNOWLEDGEMENTS

Some of these poems have appeared in:
The Irish Press; The Cork Examiner
Hibernia; The Dublin Magazine

*To Lu for twenty-five
years mutual forebearance*

CONTENTS

CONTENTS

8

CONTENTS

9

INTRODUCTION

Those who have read Alfred Allen's first book *Clashenure Skyline* will already know something of his individual mind and style, and of the landscape and heritage that bred him:

> This is the place where I was born
> This humped green country, valley torn.
> Here is my home, the only place
> Where my clothes fit me: and this race
> Of people are the people who
> Are part of the place in which I grew.
> Yet being a little unlike, apart,
> Through inbred attitudes that were part
> Of my dissenting heritage,
> My bred-out foreignness can gauge
> This country better than if I were
> Totally one with its atmosphere.

But the present collection gives a far deeper and finer idea of his talents as a writer and poet, for *Clashenure Skyline* with its collection of Irish country incidents was deliberately limited to a sharp semi-impersonality which only gave us the poet's mind in the choice and arrangement of stories, in the dark turn of a phrase, or in some double-edged passing comment on one tale or another.

Interrogations, though there is an overlap of character and atmosphere, is a very different sort of collection: for most of these poems are those of Eliot's "First voice of poetry", the voice of the poet talking to himself, or, as very often in the case of Allen's poems, arguing with himself and questioning himself in various ways. Hence the title.

11

There is seldom a striking originality of form or word, and yet there is an original strength which comes from a definite personality rooted deep in a particular place. Allen is of the breed of those strong Protestant farmers of County Cork, whose Irishness combined with otherness, whose attitudes, made up of a blending of those of gentry, farmers, and even peasantry, would make a fascinating study in itself. It is to be found in particularly vivid clash and combination West and South-West of Cork City where the planters stock has lived close to the strongest native and Gaelic tradition for centuries now.

Clashenure, where the Allens have lived for more than three hundred years, is in this countryside, on the high rounded ridge which divides the Lee to the North from its tributary the Bride to the South. Some of the old lands of Clashenure House in the Lee Valley have been lost under the new lake which now stretches for miles from the Inniscarra dam towards Macroom. Under these waters also is Innislinga Abbey which was the home of the FitzGibbons from whom Allen takes some Norman-Irish blood. The poem "Office for the Dead" shows a recurring family experience connected with Innislinga.

A farmer is rooted in the land in a particularly deep way. If it is family land, that makes it deeper still. The countryside and nature in general are not a haven of rest for the farmer as for the romantic poet, but the arena of life itself where the total personality is at grips with soil and season, plant and man and beast. Allen's poetry records such experiences ranging from high joy to black depression; and brings to his writing a restless, relentless, enquiring mind which is not afraid of some of the more terrible answers that the universe gives to those who question it closely. Waste, loss, brutality, disease and death are closer to the country-man than to most of us.

In face of the forces of life and death experienced in his world, Allen takes a tough and wary stance. He suspects that most people deliberately fool them-selves about life and death. He takes some pleasure in pricking bubbles of illusion. Irish religion, Irish politics, which have conditioned the life around him, come in for their share of deflation, but this is no mere "minority report" but rather a part of a questing and questioning attitude to human destiny. Concepts of God, of consciousness, of space and time, of life and death in man and nature, of freedom and determinism — all these work out a drama of argument in his writing.

At one end of the spectrum we have rhetorical verse of sharp debate, enjoyable for its dialectic structure but often disturbing deep layers of assumption. At the other we have what, for me, are the finest poems, which, without surrendering that sharp integrity of mind, incarnate rather than discuss experience; and, while giving us a vivid experience of the texture of physical life, leave us with a sense of both illumination and mystery. As does life itself:

> Here in an old desk drawer
> Two circlets of hair interwound
> Never exposed to the air
> Since dead hands clipped them. I found
> A note in an envelope
> "Jenny's hair and mine.
> Mine is the dark, and her loop
> The auburn hair with the shine."
>
> Fine dust, fine blown.

As he says himself Allen favours traditional stanzas and metres, and with these we find in his verse something of a literary or "poetic" vocabulary and syntax. However, these are increasingly balanced and conditioned by a personal tone — a strong individual voice rhythm, the drive of a particular mind and sensibility. In this he resembles his one acknowledged teacher, Yeats; and this is not the only likeness, for in both we also find that independence, at least partly attributable to the Protestant tradition, combined with the restless dramatisation of the Celt.

Whether he likes it or not he is a very Irish poet in almost every sense. Also like many Irish poets he seems to strengthen in imagination and technique as he gows older.

Here then in *Interrogations* is a strong individual life with as singular a flavour as the history-soaked landscape from which it grows, but which is also a commentary on the universal fates of men.

> Seán Lucy,
> Professor of Modern English,
> University College, Cork

Bride Park,
March, 1975

BORN NOT MADE

I thought myself a poet,
I dreamt my heartstrings strung,
Upon the framework of my bones,
Could sing a human song.

But when I played this fiddle,
Its songs were of the mind,
So that all I have gathered,
Is the singing of the wind.

For intellect is vapour,
The human heart is all,
And my reluctant heart strings,
Sing muted if at all.

So I am left a rhymer,
Competent at that trade,
Who follows fitful fancies
Through the mazes of the head.

ANACRONISM

I am out of tune with the times,
My poetry is rhythmical,
Even the lines end in rhymes
And the sense is quite sensible.
My attitude too is all wrong,
My ways are too temperate,
Why, I even think poetry is song
I was born too soon, or too late.

UNHELPED

I must cast all away,
The questioning of mind
Wait not for thoughts' delay,
But follow blind.
No, pathway clear and straight,
Foot after foot to follow. I was born
To go on crooked roads or none at all,
And wallow through the thorn.

MY FATHER

My father has been dead four years,
I have not written his epitaph
Time was too close. My tears
Unshed, remembered his laugh

And his story-teller's smile
Was a hurt in the mind,
I could not write it while
These were so close behind.

But time wears all things down,
I can write now of the stranger
Well loved but not well-known
In his love or in his anger.

This would be so if we lived
For a thousand thousand years,
For this lack I have grieved
Deeper than tears.

Yet he loved me I am sure
In his heart, but in his mind
I had gone a little sour
And strangely unkind.

He gave me before he died
My epitaph too in the end
"You're not a bad fellow" he said
This hurt does not mend.

For as long as I live
I'll remember this praise,
The best he could give,
He had honest ways.

Perhaps this was the reason
We never agreed,
That I was a plant out of season
Grown from old seed.

Fifty odd years are too long
Between generations of men,
New ways are always wrong,
Old ways not reverenced, then

Soldier, or sportsman, or athlete,
I was none of the things he was,
I preferred my feet
To any horse.

I took no great delight
In a strong hand,
Only mind-might
May endure to the end.

Yet he had that too I know
In his own way,
A strong intellect but narrow
And set in one way.

I have written much of myself
And little of him, and this
May be of itself
Not remiss.

For his faults are mine too,
His virtues were his own.
So I know
Now that he is gone.

He passed his judgement on me.
I pass mine on him too
He was not a bad fellow you see,
Even so.

OFFICE FOR THE DEAD

At my grandfather's death I heard
The distant music of a choir,
In broad daylight. "A singing bird",
Said others who were standing near,
"Or a clock chiming". But I knew
It was not these; it sang within
My head; it never entered through
My ears. Next day it came again
At the same time, but stronger then.

That night he died. I still can bring
That night around me, even though
I was but ten. Now what did sing
Till latterly I never knew;
I had not heard, being heretic
A monkish choir. Until one night
The glowing eye brought by its trick
That very music in the rite
Of Monks at prayer. Now on the site

Of that old house in which he died
In other times an abbey stood
Before the time of fire and sword
And he had come of ancient blood
Though it had turned heretical,
Yet Monks had once been in its debt.
Their spirits must have thought it well
To sing the Office for the dead,
To sing that Office in my head.

21

HANDIWORK

Here is my hand, see here the very nails
The same pad fingers and the self-same lines
Criss-cross the palm. I know by all the signs
This image of my own, hand in entail

Passed down the years. Now this my second son
Carries these broad-pawed tools, mine and not mine
But his, his fathers' fathers'; all that line
Carried on arms, in loins, of every one.

WISHFUL THINKING

I think if I could hold
One moment in my hand,
As when the sun was stilled
At Joshua's command,

This is the time I'd make
My one Eternity,
Just when this Autumn shook
Off Summer's mastery;

The Autumn of my life
Comes in, and I would hold
Loved children and loved wife
Stilled in this time of gold.

IN AN OLD NOTEBOOK

My second son had accidentally found
Long buried dreams of mine
In an old notebook lying around
Visions of thought and line;

Dreams of construction, budding half-baked schemes
Mostly impractical outdated now,
Dreams dreamt in longing that were only dreams
And dreams fulfilled, come true.

And this old book has a sharp bitterness
Of might have been,
Of promise unfulfilled, or something less
Than younger visions seen.

For as we age the possibilities
Narrow to what we are;
And we must mourne the lost infinities
Bound on a narrower stair.

THE DISTURBER

We have a small disturber in the house,
Busy at everything, learning how to live;
When he is quieter than a midday mouse
Then find him quickly for you'll not believe

The damage done in stealth and concentration;
But when he goes full cry upon the loose,
Then harm is done by chance, in passing on
As a tornado through the forest goes.

Climbing and falling, crying and rising up;
Climbing again, determined to be learning,
There goes the saucer followed by the cup;
Fighting outclassed, still to the fight returning.

And then he comes with hands reached out to me,
Affectionate and trusting, the Disturber,
With battered bullet-head laid on my knee
Disturbs my heart forever and forever.

CROMWELLIAN

I wonder does the dour Cromwellian dream
Of sanctimonious offspring where he lies
Nor know nor grieve at the polluted stream
Of his decayed diluted progenies.

Yet I still bear his dark fanatic blood
Pulsing intolerant in my softer veins
Dark heritage of his heart-searching mood
With me and mine unrecondite remains.

And as I age the tortured puritan
And the cold ruthlessnesses stronger grow
In my amalgam. Bigoted and vain
My bloodlines and my breeding stronger show.

Yet ten lives bridge me from his discipline
From pike and sword, and from the hangman's art
Surely a frayed attenuated line
Carries me forward from that flinty heart.

These seven spent here where calm quietness is
A single thread unbranched but interwound
With much of other threads' diversities
And mellowed by these ties of blood and ground.

Yet in my core the dour Cromwellian dreams
With all his sense of sin, driven unsure
Though but a shadow in my mind it seems
I hark back to him always, every hour.

SOURCES

I turn my intellect within my own skin,
Into the attic of my mind,
To root in dim corners musty with original sin,
And cobwebbed with old bigotries, to find

The sources of myself, and I return again
To that tumbled compilation that the Jews
Piled up through milleniums of triumph and of pain
Out of myths, revelations, prophecies, and lies.

The book that a collaboration of improbable old men
Working under the wisest fool
In Christendom, put into serviceable, plain,
Masterly, English, as a weapon and a tool

For every poet and fanatic ever since
To juggle with and batten on and use;
A murderous and glorious magnificence
Of sonorous, inaccurate, inimitable, prose

That still rings in the rafters of my mind;
And in spite of a studied lack of reverence,
Its framework is the framework that I find
Behind and beneath all my memory and sense.

THE DEAD BIRD

The blind man all alone seemed lit within
By his day's outing, sitting with his glass
At the bar-table on the home bound train,
Mocking our sight with his blind cheerfulness.

I looked out at the fields and woods of Spring;
And a begrudging pity stirred in me
For one who, listening to a sky-lark sing
Could never see it mounting up the sky.

The journey over, I, Samaritan,
Aglow with my own virtue, drove him home,
At the Asylum pushed into his hand
A crumpled note, for it was burdensome

To me, that blind men were, I sought to buy
Forgetfulness for me, some ease for them.
Ten times as much had gone that very day
On my own pleasure, but I felt no shame

Until he shook me by the hand and then
All of a sudden, kissed the hand he held;
But now I feel a queer contamination,
As if a bird had wantonly been killed.

ASHES

Oh I am bitter weary that my heart
Is barren of compassion; tinkles when struck
With icy pagan music, and is worth
No capital of love. How can I make

A warming fire when ashes fill my hearth
From pagan sacrifices, when I coldly take
Stock of the world's condition, stand apart.
No work of mercy have I undertook

But for an intellectual reasoning.
I do my brother's keeping in a book,
And make exact inglorious reckoning;
Not penetrating through the outward look
Into the inner courtyard of despair
That lies within our castle in the air.

SOLACE

If this is the solace of the dying,
This soft silly peace;
No harsh rebellions crying,
But unintelligent ease.
A dull quietness looking out of a window
At a cloud and a wheeling bird,
If these are the last things we know,
How obscenely absurd.

EPITAPH

Earth unto earth; a handful rattles down,
Ashes to ashes, on the coffin lid,
Dust unto dust, the dust of the unknown
Hides this strong spirit, as all souls are hid

That pass to silence. But this woman was
Flesh of my flesh, I find her in my bones
And in my secret mind's complexities.
On my breast too the rattle of the stones

Falls, and each falling brings a sort of death,
A weighing of life's balance farther down,
So that I breathing, feel her want of breath
And I companioned, feel like her alone.

THE INVOLVED

I know a woman beaten and abused
All the hard days her husband lived,
Ache for a blow these ten years.

I know an old man living by himself,
His gift of speech half-gone with solitude,
Mourne the shortness of loneliness.

I know a withered virgin never held
A man or child to warm her, whose one joy
Is all in penny-pinching.

I know a man who friendless, by himself,
Piles coin on coin, and thinks the days too short
For thrift, — and who shall spend?

Habit of living is most terrible:
Pray not to cling to life as these are doing,
But quit more willingly.

When you have squeezed the juices out of life
Throw out the rind.

CLAWHAMMER

Today the world has ended for a man
Whose monuments surround me and whose end
Touched me closer than I like, I can
Feel his defeat. The holes I cannot mend

In my own fabric are more prominent
For those corrupting brain and hands and eyes
That by their skill some plans of mine had lent
Substance to fulfil shadow. Now he lies

Substance becoming shadow, and I am
Something diminished in his taking off
My own concern with living seems a sham
When his has ended like a smothered cough.

The handiwork remains although the hands
Fold into interlocked quiescent bones.

FINE DUST, FINE BLOWN

Here in an old desk drawer
Two circlets of hair interwound,
Never exposed to the air
Since dead hands clipped them. I found
A note in an envelope,
"Jennie's hair and mine.
Mine is the dark, and her loop
The auburn hair with the shine".

Fine dust, fine blown.

What of these two young girls,
Cousins, and intimates,
Nothing, but these two curls,
And some letters. One letter relates
How one was jilted, and pined,
Here are the marks of her tears,
And would not become resigned,
And never knew twenty years.

Fine dust, fine blown.

The other had no such excuse,
But died of consumption too:
But that was hardly news
A hundred years ago.
Oh yes; once when I dug a grave
For an old maid who lived too long,
I found a breastplate that gave
Their date, eighteen-sixty-one.

Fine dust, fine blown.

RINGS

Friends can be taciturn. You had for me
Only the slow speech of the seasons.
Your conversation was succinct: only,
"It is Spring, it is Summer, it is Autumn,
It is Winter, I endure." This year
You bore such seed on your branches,
Pendulous to the ground from your great crown.
Did you have a premonition I wonder?
Were you trying to ensure
That the race of the weeping ash
Would survive all storms?
I last saw you alive under the storm moon
Sinisterly veiled in clouds, as a great wind
Whipped you with an abomination of all things
That obstruct the passage of negation.
I felt your agony, and was powerless.
Then in the ultimate gust of the fiercest storm of the century
You fell and splintered asunder.
All day long we have waked you
With axes and power-saws; preparing you
For your long-drawn-out funeral pyre.
Never again will we congratulate each other
On another Spring, on having survived.
You had more of them than I will have
Old friend, for I counted your rings;
And you lived two long lifetimes
As men reckon them. Yet, I am not consoled,
As with a sense of loss and vulnerability,
I warm my bum on your bones.

AN OLD WOUND

This may be why I love young trees so well:
That I have walked through stumps along these slopes
When I was young, and found unbearable
The waste of wood and beauty. I built hopes

On seeing young trees reach upwards, young boles swell
In my own lifetime. So these tapered shapes
Of larch, and spruce, and douglas, somehow heal
An old wound of neglect.

HOUSEFULL

Christmas went well for us again this year,
With candle-light and wine, with children's voices
Ringing through this old house:
And now, with midnight close,
Ghosts of ancestral memory haunt the air,
Familial ghosts, in their familiar places.

Three hundred years of ghosts come through this door,
My ghosts; I feel their spirits all around me
In doorway and on stair
Twine fingers of live air
Into my fingers. Those who trod this floor
Now feather-touch my spirit. Though I see

No shadows in the corners, yet I feel
Their seven generations pressing close.
The children's voices are
Their echoes in the air,
Ringing, alive, vibrant and youthful still,
Part of these shadows that still haunt this house.

INNOCENCE

A favoured few are given a special gift;
The quality of inborn innocence;
And all the rest of us have to make shift
With that which only comes of ignorance.

If any of that shining, chosen, few
Destroy their inner radiant quality,
They are so maimed, that everything they do
Is crippled, withered, blighted, utterly.

We are more fortunate. Our innocence
Being but an accident, is better lost.
Our bitter knowledge gives us better sense
To calculate all dangers, count all cost.

We who were never chosen, are therefore free
To choose the comfort of complacency.

VERTIGO

Grim shadows in the mind's dark rooms
Infect with vertigo our secret dreams.

EGO

Deep in the mind lies the inscrutable egg,
Resilient, shiny: this the inner I,
Containing the unknown of boon or plague,
Content in black oblivion to lie.

Yet I would fondle it against its will
With all the feeling fingers of the mind,
And press its toughened blackness, and be still
Till it resumes its smooth, unwrinkled, bland

And plump rotundity. Tempted to crush
Until it bursts like puff-ball under foot.
Then all intricacies would outward rush,
All things in panic from the dying root,

Rush in a frenzy of unknit delight,
The fragments flying in eternal night.

JOURNEY INTO PERPLEXITY

Our intellect has pushed the mists away
One inch before our eyes: only so far
That the opaque can mirror our dismay
At seeing what we are.

COMPUTER

This abacus is an atom
Of the scum on a bubble
That strives for self-knowledge,
And gets for its trouble,
As it moves from the edge
To the heart of its home,
But advanced electronics
Instead of a soul;
Mere mechanical tricks,
A console to console.

How then to recover
From the sick state it's in?
But wire itself up
For original sin;
And conjure up hope
When this lifetime is over
Of the endless switch-clicks
Of Eternity-role;
Immortal electrics,
Mechanical soul?

PRIDE OF CREATION

The Fall of Lucifer's the key to all
That lies entangled between womb and grave;
For all creation hinges on His Fall;
That act of pride compelling God to live

To counteract that pride. His overthrow
Spread out the burning stars beneath His hand;
And He grew prouder that each atom knew
How He had bound it into time. This bond

Forged by His Fall, is still immutable,
Cannot be broken, unless all sinks down
Into the stillness that before the Fall
Made up the oneness of oblivion.

For this indeed is Lucifer's offence,
That being aware, He broke the Infinite Silence.

EQUATION

All things are one, and the answer is no,
This is a strong un-faith.
All things are unity, and they go
Nowhere, to nothing, too late.

Both sides of the problem solve to this
X + OO = I.
The total sum of a million times yes
Is no, and nothing, and none.

RUNAWAY

Man's mind unbridled gallops down the road
Of Science ever faster, and the goad
That spurs it is that itching in the blood
That has been burning there since man began
To look for cause in an effect, since then
Man has been itching not for right or good.

Only for knowledge, knowledge creates power;
Pursuit of power has been the constant spur
That drives the intellect to ever more
Invention and discovery, and these
Are self perpetuating; they increase
Out of themselves: now that this Babel-tower

Looms to the stars, foundation fast in Hell,
A manic beanstalk mushroom-growing still
To Lucifer's high landing whence he fell,
Let us direct itself upon itself to find
The reason for this growing tower of mind
That obscures Heaven and all things spiritual.

Greece was the start of it; the first clear mind
Was Greek: before it all was hallowed, blind,
Instinctive and accepting. This new kind
Of intellect was smothered under Christ
Until the Reformation floodtide burst
The bounds of order: set each man to find

His own interpretation. From thence on
Science has been the Godhead of those men
Who mould the World with thought and action.
This little leaven that transcends the beast
In all our human lump, waxed and increased
In strict proportion as the lump has grown.

And their first fruits of knowledge multiplied
Mankind, scattered it far and wide,
And kept alive the multitudes who died
In other ages, and in spite of War
Famine, and pestilence, increased the power
Of massed intelligence. On every side.

More minds are trained, less genius is concealed
In ignorance, Man the precocious child,
Entranced with what his candle has revealed,
Juggles with knowledge-fire to light the dark
Of all material mystery. One spark
Could light a flare to burn up his world.

But what if luck attends him, if the fire
Remains his servant, building up his power?
What if man's intellect be made to soar
Beyond the stars? Be made to circumvent
Time and its variant distance, these being bent
To mankind's purpose, what can man do more.

Then carry his inherent load of fear
Of guilt and doubt, on upwards with his tower?
A mental giant in a moral sewer?
He still must make the longest voyage of all
Clear-eyed into the dark: answer the call
Of Death imperative the all-vanquisher.

For every man must make one voyage alone,
Whether within the orbit of this sun
Or beyond Betelgeuse all secrets won
Of space and time and distance, no one shares
That last aloneness. All his hopes and fears
Thereby fall silent, and his soul goes on.

Goes whither? Science answer if you can
Of God of practicality, whence man,
And whither when this comedy is done?
Out in far blackness powdered with dim stare
The individual taken unawares
Must die as died his fathers, quite alone.

SPACEMEN OR SPECIMEN

The still immaculate moon rides up the sky
On this December night;
In this plucked second of Eternity
That is our apex, we can finally
Marry touch to our sight.

But what does Aphrodite care for us,
Mankind the may-fly god?
She who was sunk in sleep before our race
Flicked into life on her companion's face,
And will be still abed

When we are reunited with the dark
What other questing ships
Sank on her cold indifference, whose mark
Is now but darker mark upon her dark.
Their race long in eclipse

And when the winds blow over Earth again,
Empty, and cold, and free,
Over each dried-up ocean, dusty plain,
Will there come voyaging from that boundless Main
Some others such as we?

PARADOX

Nothing faster than light?
But the law that we know
Governs its flight
Must precede its glow.
For how else can it
Be where the waves flow
Or anticipate
Where the light has to go?

THE LOST INFINITIES

What force pulsed through that dark and timeless night
To form the framework of the natural laws
Layer upon layer, that bind the Universe
So that however deep we look for light
Of answering reason, that primeval cause
Retreats behind another calculus?

What purpose had that force, to what far end
Did it spin out those countless stars through space,
Which since they burn cannot be infinite
In time or numbers, for the very blend
That harbours time, by harbouring it must force
All time-formed things back into formless night?

Evolve, the great command to all that moves;
That made the formless night congeal, cohere,
Into the nebulae, the stars, this Earth,
This narrow stage on which we live our lives:
But to what purpose the long war that here
Brought mankind through the ages to the birth

Of speculative reason? Where to now?
What supercedes us in finality?
How many steps remain until the end?
What meaning has this end to which we go?
What is the ultimate reality?
Does God down all the ages seek a friend

Like to Himself? The pitiless great heart
Of all existence using lack of ruth
To form in this queer manner, something sib,
Something akin, to what was at the start,
As greatly infinite a lonely truth?
Are we indeed perhaps Great Adam's rib?

BEWILDERMENT

No creed that man has held explains the wild
Bewildered sobbing of a tortured child,
No twisted image of a God of love
Can make that suffering meaningful. I rave
Deep in the heart against a God of light
Who suffers suffering within his sight,
Nor can a God of justice ever be
Acceptable by reasoning to me,
If there is something meaningful, then what
What purpose and what object has God got?
No creed is to be found that can explain
Disease, injustice, hunger, torture, pain.
They say God's purpose lies beyond our knowing,
What crop does He expect from such a sowing?

LAZARUS AND DIVES

If nothing but happiness
Afflicts the saved souls in Heaven,
Then what of the bitter distress
Of Lazarus in Abraham's bosom,
Condemned for ever and ever
To watch damned Dives choking
Of thirst, while the glittering river
Of Paradise gurgles by mocking?

CURRENT AFFAIRS

Can it be possible to bring alive
A God by much believing? Perhaps faith
Can breathe reality into a myth
If men enough, for long enough, believe.

If enough worshipping brings forth a God,
Perhaps those generations that believed
Made Christ be retrospectively conceived;
By faith created the Christ crucified?

Does faith still dye the Virgin's mantle blue?
And would it fade, if all that hailing died?
Have all the Gods that men have glorified
Vanished, when their believers grew too few?

Or is the ghost of Zeus real enough;
Like an appliance, when the current's off?

REVULSION

You ask what I detest the most
While conscious between dust and dust,
I answer, Nature's pointless waste.

The way death visits anywhere,
The mutilations and the fear
That even children have to bear,

The things that but exist to prey
On living bodies inwardly
Which die when those they prey on die,

The pain of loving through it all,
The way the sparrows always fall,
The separateness of every soul,

The hectic beauty of the Earth,
The random happenstance of birth
That still works out a plan set forth

By some dim purpose in the past,
Some dream of some absenting ghost,
These are the things I hate the most.

THE LILIES OF THE FIELD

Consider the lilies of the field;
They toil not, neither do they spin;
But their beauty of blossom has concealed
Their quota of original sin.

For like all things that live and that die,
They work and they worry and they fight;
And they grapple with their roots, and they try
To steal from their neighbours in the night;

Brother contending with brother
For moisture and soil and sun;
Each trying to smother the other,
For life lives by death alone.

So consider the lilies; oh consider,
Carefully consider them indeed;
Consider that flowers as they wither
Carefully conserve their seed;

And that aeons of fierce competition,
Whose ferocious culmination is man,
Have made an overriding condition
Of survival, since the World began.

Now that man far surpasses the lily
In competing for soil and for sun,
The question arises, now will he
Still do what the lilies have done.

HEY-LINKUM-LARUM

All frogs need storks. Luther was surely right;
For if frogs dream, they can't but know this well
Since dreams and dreamers coexist with night
Like frogs and storks with ponds. The Sirens' call

Compels because along with ecstasy
It proffers dissolution. In that dream
There comes an end of dreaming. When the sky
Becomes too vast for frogs, the siren gleam

In a stork's eye shines like the lode-stone star
To draw them to that beak of destiny,
Entranced and terror-stricken. For they are,
Like all God's creatures, sure, that finally

Surrender to their storks awaits them all:
For frogs and storks are born in mutual thrall.

THE ANIMAL

Imagination is the curse,
That Adam got with apple-seed.
For dreams are knowledge gone perverse
They father souls; the thorn and weed.

Grow in these souls and not in Eden.
The Angel with the fiery sword
Burns in the heart, and that is when
Man becomes man, from Eden barred.

Yet if we live the life of sensation,
The pleasant sensation, the easy time,
The days of comfort and satisfaction,
Humdrum and unsublime.

Then the animal takes over,
The pig in us grunts and wallows,
The cow groans in the clover,
The air caresses the swallows

Then life is a moment lived alone
No past and no future. A spot of light
Travels our pathway. Unlit and unknown,
All behind and before us, deep in dark night,

Better to suffer a thousand times
The pains of hell with all the burnings,
Than to live without the secret of rhymes,
And imaginations twists and turnings.

Mere animalness is the price of ease;
The barren born of unconsciousness
This is the penalty of peace,
Better by far life's bitterness.

ENGINEER'S REPORT

In working order, heavy duty model,
One major overhaul by first-class firm.
Should give good service if not overdriven,
In which case guarantee would be invalid,
All such excesses being at owner's risk.

Although neglected by the present owner,
Should remain good for years if well looked after,
Being programmed for some curious applications,
Adapted for some quite unusual duties,
Should give good service if not overstressed.

Opinion is he would be ill-advised to
Dispose of it at present, quite outside of
The sentimental, since he can't replace it;
But he is warned that there will come a moment
When it must finally become just scrap.

Meanwhile, he probably will still neglect it,
Use incorrect lubricants and grades of fuel;
Couplings grown slack will not be checked or serviced.
Sometimes, on sleepless nights, the pump turns over
Lumpily, as in incipient malfunction.

VULNERABILITY

No soul today inviolable
The martyr singing in the fire is gone,
Science has beaten him, Science is able
To break and build the soul of everyone.

The hollow needle and a new technique,
These have unmanned the strongest, without scar
On their unbroken bodies, none unique,
All brains are washable, all souls must fear.

All souls were proud, if only one remained
Unbreakable, its own, whatever came.
But now when everyone can be retrained,
All souls are in the dust, all are in shame.

Image of Godhead? No, not one of these,
When they can bend and shape them as they please.

THE CAGE

The beaten leaves
Revile the wind,
And the wind grieves,
World without end.

Impent alone
I batter my cage
I cannot atone
For the world's rage.

I stretch my being
To my fingers' ends
Still without seeing
Any amends.

The heart alone
Solves no riddle
The tone
Is not the fiddle.

At its worst
When most giving,
The mind has cursed
All living.

The long blight
Still falls,
Man's might
Is his prison walls.

The withered grass
Reviles the sun,
All things pass,
And are gone.

THE DRIVING WIND

That great and lonely crying in the wind,
Sings of great forces indiscriminate
Endlessly wandering by certain fate
Foreshadowed at beginning by their end.

So with all living things, for when the first
Coagulate amoeba doubled up,
We had already drunk of that great cup
Known all our shadings of the best and worst.

So all souls sing within the driving wind
And all the singers have become the song
Sung at the start, the middle and the end
Of that great stream that carries us along,
Who then can mumble of the late or soon,
Or where that timeless singing was begun?

DUCKS AND DRAKES

The wheat ears rustling, the wind-torn clouds,
Sun through an evening shower,
The wild-fowl hurtling in knotted crowds
Swing up, swing round, swing lower.

The wave-tops gathering the glittering light,
Shrillness of hilltop air,
The rainbow wandering and dazzling sight,
All things vivid and rare.

Action and death — the colour of blood;
Mallard swing into range,
The thud on the earth, and the purpose of God
Changeless in constant change.

SPRING

Spring is here again,
That young old thing,
Wearily the world's pain,
Brings back Spring.

The child with the old face
Runs down the lanes;
Running the same race,
To the same ends.

Because the earth canted
Aslant as it spun.
All life is jointed
To the pulse of the sun.

So wearily the seasons
Come, and come again
In repetitive processions,
Repetitive refrain.

And Spring is a young thing,
With an old face,
That can neither lose or win
The predestined race.

So Spring is here again
So what? We've seen it all.
There is much pain,
In the cuckoo-call.

And the warmth in the sun,
Goes to the bone.
I count Springs gone,
My heart like a stone.

DOWNWIND

I know the seasons by the barley smell,
Spring is raw earth, with green spears thrusting through,
The Summer muskiness I know so well
Pervades the moonlit dusk, scenting the dew,

When trees are all in leaf, and insect-hum
Vibrates the golden air, the feather-sheen
Of new-eared tender barley sighs, then come
Waves of that heavy fragrance from that green

And whispering restless sea; that promises
The golden ripening, and the harvest moon,
Ducks flighting in the dusk, the harmonies
Of man and nature through the season-run.

While Wintertime has the best scent of all
The malt-tang that I know and love so well.

JANUARY

I ache for Spring in January's wild weather,
In rending wind, and cloud-entangled moon,
With snow and sleet in burning showers together,
I ache for April, and the cuckoo-tune.

Clear in calm evening above greener grass
And leaves of startling tenderness. I long
For warmth in sun, and clouds that pass
Through the clear blue, when light is sharp and strong

And all things glow with hope. For these I ache
With forty years' nostalgias. I must take
More notice as the precious years unwind,

For greater age has made me understand
How fast the life-line flickers from the hand.

DAWN BIRD

Lifting his head,
Opening his throat,
His stupid song
The selfsame note.

His fathers had
Since birds were birds
Same three notes,
Same three words.

Outside my window
Up in a tree,
The dawn bird sings
Disgustingly.

VIXEN

The vixen calls, and in her tears
The message of a million years,
Night-crying on the wind.

Now all at once the household curs
Yammer resentment to the stars,
Envy and hatred blend.

They cannot know what they have lost,
Yet in their hearts they feel the cost
Of being man's friend.

CATHERINE-WHEEL

Almost November now, with broken weather
Bird-and-leaf-haunted skies, and drifts of rain:
Sun, eye, and water prisming together,
Breed broken rainbows, Winter comes again.

DECEMBER LIGHT

The wind-enscalloped water, black not blue
Under December's sun, white flecked, impelled
And over it the birds wind-driven too,
Flung in the air, flung far and held

By their wing-competence from only being
Blown flotsam in the air. The wild geese call,
All wildness in their chanting on the wing,
While easily the gulls above them sail;

And on the Winter-wasted lake's hill-ring
The suns obliqueness throws a winter light,
A sullen sparkle while bare bushes sing
Of the Wind's mindlessness in endless flight,

And in high desolation in the blue
White pencil-mark of jet drawn straight and true.

THE HERON

End of a day, when night and twilight blend:
End of a life; lives are as grains of sand:
End of a frog; of frogs there is no end:
The heron's beak impales the sunset pond.

Grey hunter, patient for my little fish,
Meanwhile make do with frogs, then stand quite still
Hunched in the water; heron make your wish
And dip, and dip again, and eat your fill.

That pitiless and patient watchful eye;
That ghostly scream; that ponderousness of wing;
Those rudder feet projecting as you fly;
That pointed beak, so ready weaponing;

Bird of the forest, killer, wary one,
Stand, and be patient for the rising moon.

THE STAIRWAY

An ear of wheat upon the palm, now twist
The heel of hand upon it, and you have
The heart of living; hand of chaff and grist
Refutes the wisdom of the pastoralist.

Here in your hand the stairway to the stars
Had its first landing, when man bound a sheaf
He started all of that, cities and wars
Learning and wondering, dark, thoroughfares

Lined by dark doorways of the hidden mind
That have bright secrets of the world to give.
God grant that settled living grows not blind,
Nor patterned to the ant-hill, but will find

Itself upon the stairway of the sheaf,
Still reaching upwards for the unconfined.

HERITAGE

This is an ancient land, and in it still
Is felt the pull of older generations,
Nor is there any valley, any hill,
Which has not known in its configurations

Old struggle and old loss remembered yet,
If by none other than the very ground
That carries to the nostrils yet a breath
Of age-old things. For every single mound

Is redolent of past, and old ways dead
Past all reviving, not past grieving for
Now while we turn to tread the way ahead
Let us remember those who went before

For all our antecedents press us on,
This land of ours was moulded by their being,
All those who came to steal it one by one
Are mingled in it. We are all one thing,

And all the ghosts of all the years gone by
Are all our ghosts. Nor are there many now
Can say "My blood is pure", our ancestry
Is bastardised in race. Not any bough

Of all our tree can say "I am a pure",
Irish or Englishman, Norman or Dane,
In our dissensions we can now be sure,
The victor's throat shouts forth the victim's pain.

77

For I have seen the Pict upon the frame
Of the gaunt Norman knight, his sallow face
Stamped with a Celtic dream. This very same
Saxon by chance of name. I know a race

Of Norman patronymic with the nose
Of a sea wanderer of long ago
Proud as a trireme's prow. When in repose
This face has ancient pride Carthage would know.

We gather the four winds into our loins
Wave after wave has mingled in our sea,
All that was separate, together joins
To make the Irish people, you and me,

That queer amalgam that insists to boast
Of ancient grandeurs that were seldom there.
Of ancient cities that were thatch and post,
Their grandest edifice a stark round tower.

Better by far to think of what we are,
A people flung upon the winds, a part
Of other better, greater, things by far,
One age has finished, and new ages start.

CARITAS

The love of man precludes the love of men:
A paradox that may indeed explain
Why Christ was not a socialist, and why
All ideologists lack humanity.

THE OLD MAN OF THE MOUNTAINS

That troubled crossroads where convictions meet
Revives a myth. Does some far-fetched Old Man
Reign on a Syrian mountain once again
As grim dispenser of selective death?

A passionate hysteria of hate
Consumed the heart that drove the bullet in;
But who indoctrinated the assassin?
Who promised him eternal wild delight?

Worth every punishment? In long past days
Hashish and tricks, and holy mysteries
Brought paradise before his very eyes

Complete with houris. In this modern hour
Hashish is pot, the houri is a whore,
Old Men infest the mountains everywhere.

THE SIGHTLESS

I

Blind Samson when the house is down
Will you have eyes to see
The walls piled up on everyone
Each broken enemy.

How many like you always will
Grope blindly at the heart
Of ordered life, arms tensed to pull
The settled world apart

No plague has ever seen that it
Lacks logic at the last
For when its triumph is complete
Then all its power is past

The plague is dead. Without a host
All that mad hatred too is lost.

II

Oh questioner, my burning pride
Makes me taste such a gall
That blind I pull on every side
On pillar and on wall.

And though I only break one house
I break it from within
And others like me, this will rouse
To break up one by one

Your treasured store of hoarded things
Your wisdom, beauty, power
Oh what an ecstasy this brings
This vengeful Godlike hour.

Powerless to build, I'll surely raze
Making all sick with my malaise.

III

Do you expect when all is down
Blind Samson, there will rise
Out of the ruins, for everyone
A Greater Paradise

Then you're a fool, a devil's fool
For men will have to start
Foundation upwards, when you pull
The settled world apart

And you will never see one brick
Set up upon another
Being only skilled in how to wreck
How can men call you brother

And your inheritors will be
A new, and harsher, hierarchy.

IV

What do I care for that, I feel
My sinews growing strong
Again with grinding at the mill
My hair is loosed and long

Since the hot iron took my sight
When I was shorn, betrayed
By one I loved. But now my might
Will be again displayed

And my hate will be satisfied
In the down-crashing wall
And sighted eyes are nullified
When darkness falls on all

Though bright and lustrous in the head
What good are eyeballs to the dead?

V

Blind Samson, now the house is down
Say, with your last, hard breath
Facing, like everyone, alone
The emptiness of death

What did it profit you, that pull
That broke the world apart
Revenge is dead, and hell is full
And emptied quite the heart

New view with borrowed eyes, the vast
Eternal endless sea
Where both the future and the past
Are both content to be

And where both bright and blinded eyes
All glaze together as light dies.

ANCESTRAL VOICES

An Orangewoman ranting on the air,
Passionately mindless, mindlessly passionate,
Belfast's Cassandra prophesying war,
Hysterical and lunatic with hate.

A flag-draped coffin and a last hurrah
For Shakespeare's Ingineer; but Shakespeare's sport
Excites no laughter when there's children there.
In God's name what is Ireland's freedom worth?

Epics must not be written any more.
Never again the tribute of a song
To warrior-heroes, for Troy's flame-wrapped tower
Is shown for what it has been all along.

Heroes are simpletons. A Bogside boy
Drunk and delirious, throwing petrol-bombs,
Is of a kind with those who looted Troy,
And Orange zealots lie in gold-bright tombs

With Agamemnon. Heroes, heroes all,
Barren of anything but hate and blood.
How did Achilles gain by Hector's fall?
How did the world gain? What was the good?

ULYSSES

In this long now they seem like dreaming things,
All those adventures, all my craftiness,
All that deep feeling. Scent and taste and touch
All untrustworthy. Think, why should a rose
Scent, and a carcase stink? This mystery
Of scent and stench, of ecstasy and agony
As yet remains unsolved, here among Shades.
What does it matter now the flesh is gone?
A Spirit neither smells, nor tastes, nor touches.
Hearing and sight are all the senses left
Beyond corruption; so a Shade may be
Spectator, auditor, and nothing more.
Two out of five: and yet we grow another
Sharper than either, and this sixth insists
That matter is a dream, and that reality
Is of this place of Shades, horizonless.
But yet, the dream was good. I taste the wine
Remembered in Eternity. And women's arms,
And men's arms in the tumult before Troy,
The skilful carpentry that made the horse,
And how we lay within it, waiting, waiting;
All these were good, and it was better still
To step ashore after my wandering years,
Grizzled, alone, but still the warrior,
To find Penelope, older, but faithful.
I'd had my flighty bits; I settled down.
Yes, this was good, and good my wanderings.
I used my body as birds use their wings.

HELEN

I had a high adventure in my dream.
It seems a swan came at the start of it.
I always loved the feel of downy things
So I'll not question Leda's lame excuse,
Swansdown is worn by Princes, why not Gods?
Yet some great destiny informed my dreaming.
I pulled a thousand ships about my ears.
(How else can women matter in a world
Warrior-dominated?) I discovered lust,
But what is love? What is that mystery
That common people know? It seems it is
Savoured in, flavoured by, obscurity.
This I have missed. They say the whole being sings.
I crave a body as a bird craves wings.

ACHILLES

My dream was but a glint upon a sword,
A quick reflection on the mirror-bronze,
Soon blood-eclipsed. The quickness of my eye
Strength and agility and arrogance,
And courage quite unflawed, were all I had.
For the false fable of my tender heel
Gives me less credit than is really due.
My dream holds draughty tents upon the shore
And a loved boy who died a needless death.
It holds the dust and blood where Hector died
Vengeance for my own fault. My thoughts since then
Carry a bitter twist. Now, in the Shades,
I'm still the warrior. What can warriors do
But fight, and so I issue challenges
To others of my kind, a heroes' band,
Who dreamt before me or dreamt afterward.
And some of them have been most strangely armed:
One, with an ass's jawbone; some with spears;
Others with tubes of fire. They come, they go,
I am the master still; although one grim,
Dark, crooked-featured, dour, and bitter one,
With whom a raven flew. — But what of him,
I had grown careless, and my sandal slipped.
I have no wound: but then we never wound;
The sword goes through and we are whole again.
No blood, no pain, no death. How can there be
When we have neither feeling, taste nor touch,
Nor any substances more than shadow has?
What use my vaunted skill and valour then

When I am not at risk? Courage in limbo
Is meaningless. What though the sword-blade sings?
I crave a body as a bird craves wings.

HECTOR

All my loud shouting was a counterfeit
Drummed up to nerve my arm. I was no fierce
Lover of slaughter. I bought courage dear.
Yet I had skill and strength, and only feared
One man among them all, one fatal one,
And I was not deceived by arms or armour.
I feared him for his single-mindedness
That focused all his being in his sword,
And all that sword into its needle point.
There were too many facets to my being;
Heir to a kingdom, husband, general,
And father above all. I was diverse;
My points were many. So it was I died.
I still can feel my eyeballs full of sand
As I was dragged heel-first about the walls:
That was the latest thing I ever felt.
What happened to my children and my wife
When the horse opened I have yet to know.
This Hades is so huge, only a chance
Of chances would inform me. What's the odds,
For surely all are dust, and are as I
Long finished with the dream; with mortal things.
Why should I crave a body? Why crave wings?

MENELAUS

Most of my dream was nightmarish indeed,
The nightmare of obsession. I, obsessed,
Spent men and ships, and wasted priceless years,
Trying to reclaim that which I never had.
For when I held bright Helen in my arms,
Before, – and more than ever afterwards,
I never touched the secret of possession,
No, no, not once, despite the children bred.
Was there some want in me, was there in her
Some strangeness? Once, I thought I felt
Soft down upon her body. Feathers, feathers,
And sometimes she hissed softly in her sleep.
No matter, when she went, I moved the earth,
Tirelessly, patiently, stirred up the Greeks,
Exploited all their jealousy and fear,
Their greed and their resentment against Troy.
And men would say that I had good success:
Troy to the flames, and Paris to the sword,
And Helen mine again, I had these things,
I had her body, but her soul had wings.

PARIS

My dreaming whim destroyed ten thousand dreams
To build a legend. Helen was a prize,
A feather in my cap. And I to her?
Escape from brutishness? Escape to what?
They say that she was fathered by a swan.
I only know her mother was a shrew,
And she her most true daughter. Of all things
The high romantic is most difficult
To keep continually at fever-pitch.
Helen, the heroine, was my ten year's bane.
Indeed, I quit the dream most willingly.
Death has its terrors, but it set me free
From all her postures, all her bitter stings.
She was the bird, so let her have the wings.

AGAMEMNON

The incident was fortunate for me.
What pretext could serve better against Troy?
I needed war. Tyrants must have a war,
A nice, safe, distant, war, fought overseas.
Won, I had won it; lost, the Greeks had lost,
And I would sorrow with them. Either way
I stood to gain, but victory was better.
It broke the Trojan stranglehold on trade,
And there was booty. So I was well pleased
Homecoming to Mycenae. That's the joke.
God give me hands, and give her throat to choke.
God, how I wish we both were living beings.
I crave it as a broken bird craves wings.

PRIAM

I was the loser, both as man and king.
The magic of my office atrophied,
All those I loved were slaughtered or enslaved,
All that I loved was levelled and destroyed.
My own small death I reckon not at all:
We all must die; but I betrayed my trust
In that I failed to keep the kingdom safe.
I hunger for oblivion, memory clings.
Where would I fly if I were given wings?

CASSANDRA

I warned them, that's the least that can be said,
I gave fair warning; but I'd warned too much,
And people tire of warnings, run perverse
Headlong upon calamity. Perhaps I'd loved
Warning too much, and revelled in each doom.
If I had warned less often, when I warned,
They would have listened; but then great events
Are seldom born except in trivial things.
I always was a Shade. What use are wings?

HOMER

You ask me was it real, this tale I told.
I tell you that I put the flesh on bones.
Sightless, I saw more grandeur than there was.
Helen eloped, and ships did sail for Troy:
Hector, and Achilles, and others fought,
And Troy did burn. These were the bones I used,
But were the dreams heroic? Gods and men,
As I saw gods and men, are of my dream.
They are my children, fathered on those others,
Those ignorant, brutish, cruel, and savage others,
Who gave my tale a shape. I need no wings.
I crave no body. My dream soars and sings.